A Benjamin Blog
and His Inquisitive Dog
Guide

Egypt

Anita Ganeri

Heinemann
LIBRARY

Chicago, Illinois

© 2015 Heinemann Library
an imprint of Capstone Global Library, LLC
Chicago, Illinois

Edited by Dan Nunn, Helen Cox Cannons, and Gina Kammer
Designed by Jo Hinton-Malivoire
Picture research by Ruth Blair and Hannah Taylor
Production by Helen McCreath
Originated by Capstone Global Library Ltd
Printed and bound in China by Leo Paper Group

18 17 16 15 14
10 9 8 7 6 5 4 3 2 1

Library of Congress
Cataloging-in-Publication Data
Cataloging-in-publication information is on file with the Library of Congress.
ISBN 978-1-4109-6663-6 (hardcover)
ISBN 978-1-4109-6672-8 (paperback)
ISBN 978-1-4109-6690-2 (eBook PDF)

Acknowledgments
We would like to thank the following for permission to reproduce photographs:

Alamy: Andrew Woodley, 16, Banana Pancake, cover, Barry Iverson, 9, Christine Osborne Pictures, 21, Egypt/Janzig, 19, Horizon International Images Ltd., 25, Ivan Vdovin, 7, Middle East, 6, Simon Reddy, 20, Travelshots.com/Peter Phipp, 26; Corbis: Hemis/Arnaud Chicurel, 24; Getty Images: Clive Mason, 22, David Sutherland, 15, Hisham Ibrahim, 13, Juergen Ritterbach, 12, Justin Minns, 11, Shanna Baker, 4, UIG/Majority World, 17, Wael Hamdan, 18, Wayne Walton, 14; Newscom: Reuters/Mohamed Abd El Ghany, 23; Shutterstock: Bart Acke, 10, Boris Stroujko, 8, Globe Turner, 28, sculpies, 27, 29

007017LEOF14

Some words are shown in bold, **like this.** You can find out what they mean by looking in the glossary.

Contents

Welcome to Egypt!

Hello! My name is Benjamin Blog and this is Barko Polo, my **inquisitive** dog. (He is named after ancient ace explorer, **Marco Polo**.) We have just gotten back from our latest adventure—exploring Egypt. We put this book together from some of the blog posts we wrote on the way.

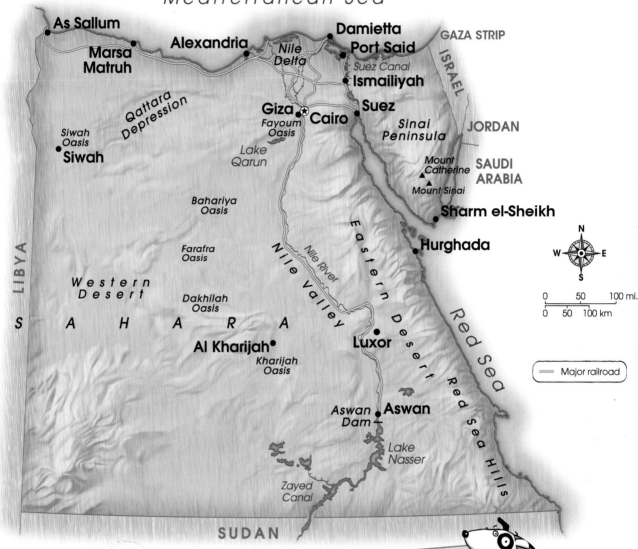

Egypt
Topographical map

Mediterranean Sea

As Sallum
Marsa Matruh
Alexandria
Nile Delta
Damietta
Port Said
GAZA STRIP
Suez Canal
ISRAEL
Ismailiyah
Qattara Depression
Giza
Fayoum Oasis
Cairo
Suez
Sinai Peninsula
JORDAN
Siwah Oasis
Siwah
Lake Qarun
Mount Catherine
Mount Sinai
SAUDI ARABIA
Bahariya Oasis
Sharm el-Sheikh
Farafra Oasis
Eastern Desert
Hurghada
W e s t e r n   D e s e r t
Nile Valley
Nile River
LIBYA
S A H A R A
Dakhilah Oasis
Al Kharijah
Kharijah Oasis
Luxor
Red Sea
Red Sea Hills
Aswan Dam
Aswan
Lake Nasser
Zayed Canal
SUDAN

N
W E
S

0   50   100 mi.
0   50   100 km

⎯ Major railroad

BARKO'S BLOG-TASTIC EGYPT FACTS
Egypt is a large country in northern Africa. It has coastlines with the Mediterranean Sea and the Red Sea. On land, it is joined to Libya, Sudan, Israel, and the Gaza Strip.

Ancient Egypt

Posted by: Ben Blog | February 3 at 10:03 a.m.

Our first stop was the Valley of the Kings near the city of Luxor. This is where the bodies of some of the rulers of ancient Egypt were buried in **tombs** cut into the cliffs. I am off to visit the tomb of Tutankhamun.

BARKO'S BLOG-TASTIC EGYPT FACTS

In the 600s, the religion of **Islam** reached Egypt. Many **mosques** were built where **Muslims** (followers of Islam) could worship. This is the ancient mosque of Ibn Tulun, which was built in the 800s.

From Dry Deserts to Long Rivers

Posted by: Ben Blog | February 5 at 2:35 p.m.

From Luxor, we drove west into the desert. It covers two-thirds of Egypt and is dry, sandy, and baking hot. I managed to find an **oasis**. This is a place where water springs up from underground. Barko took this snapshot of me standing under a shady date palm. Phew!

BARKO'S BLOG-TASTIC EGYPT FACTS

The highest mountain in Egypt is Mount Catherine. It stands 8,625 feet (2,629 meters) tall. Next door is the slightly shorter Mount Sinai. It is a holy place for Christians, Jews, and **Muslims**.

Next, we hopped on a sailing boat called a **felucca** for a trip along the Nile River. The Nile is the longest river on Earth. It flows for around 4,132 miles (6,650 kilometers) from Lake Victoria in central Africa through Egypt to the Mediterranean Sea. The river is an important water supply, and most people in Egypt live along its banks.

BARKO'S BLOG-TASTIC EGYPT FACTS
The Red Sea is part of the Indian Ocean and is famous for its extraordinary **coral reefs**. More than 1,200 types of fish live in the sea, along with hundreds of crabs, jellyfish, shellfish, turtles, and dolphins. I think I will take a quick dip and have a look.

City Tour

We have arrived in Cairo, the capital city of Egypt, which is spread out along the Nile River. More than 9 million people live here, making it one of the biggest cities in Africa. I am here in one of the city's **souks**, doing some souvenir shopping.

BARKO'S BLOG-TASTIC EGYPT FACTS

Egypt's second-largest city is Alexandria, which is located in the north along the Mediterranean coast. The city is around 2,300 years old and is Egypt's biggest **port**.

Salaam Alaikum!

While we are in Egypt, I thought that I would take some Arabic lessons. Arabic is the official language of Egypt, and most Egyptians speak it. *Salaam alaikum* means "peace to you." *Ezzayak* means "How are you?" Arabic is written and read from right to left.

14

BARKO'S BLOG-TASTIC EGYPT FACTS
These people are Bedouins who live in the Egyptian desert. They live in tents and travel from place to place. They wear long, flowing robes to keep them cool.

Most Egyptians live in cities. Many people are very poor and live in cramped, overcrowded homes.
I am here in the countryside, visiting a village. The people here live in simple, mud-brick houses and work as farmers, growing crops and raising sheep and goats.

BARKO'S BLOG-TASTIC EGYPT FACTS

In Egypt, children start school when they are 6 years old. Education is free, but many children from poor families have to leave school early to work or help on the farm.

Today, we are back in Cairo to visit this amazing **mosque**. Most people in Egypt are **Muslims** and follow the religion of **Islam**. A mosque is a building where Muslims go to meet and worship. This mosque stands on top of a hill and can be seen from many miles away.

BARKO'S BLOG-TASTIC EGYPT FACTS

Some people in Egypt are Coptic Christians. They worship in churches. This church in Cairo is called the Hanging Church because it is built above an ancient gateway.

19

Time for Lunch

Posted by: Ben Blog | May 2 at 1:15 p.m.

After a busy morning, we stopped for lunch. I picked kushari, a typical Egyptian dish. It is made from rice, lentils, and pasta, topped with tomato sauce and sprinkled with crispy fried onions. At home, it is often cooked to use up leftovers at the end of the month. Cool idea!

BARKO'S BLOG-TASTIC EGYPT FACTS

You can buy many tasty snacks from street stalls, such as this one. Falafel are made from mashed beans or chickpeas, rolled into a ball and fried. They are delicious in **pita bread**.

Soccer and films

Staying in Cairo, we headed to the Cairo Stadium to watch a soccer match between the top two teams in Egypt—Al Ahly and Zamalek. Soccer is the most popular sport in Egypt, and when important matches are played, the country comes to a standstill.

BARKO'S BLOG-TASTIC EGYPT FACTS

Egyptian people like going to the movies in their spare time. Thousands of films have been made in Egypt. People also like listening to music and watching **soap operas** on TV.

From Tourists to Canals

Our next stop was the city of Sharm el-Sheikh, on the Red Sea coast. After the hustle and bustle of Cairo, we needed a good rest. Sharm el-Sheikh is very popular with tourists who come to snorkel, scuba dive, swim, and sunbathe. I think I will have a quick nap first.

BARKO'S BLOG-TASTIC EGYPT FACTS

The Suez Canal is 101 miles (163 kilometers) long. It links the Mediterranean Sea and the Red Sea and is a shortcut between Europe and Asia. Before the canal was built, ships had to sail a very long way around the tip of Africa.

And Finally ...

These are the amazing temples of Abu Simbel. We are here on the last day of our tour. What an awesome sight. They were carved out of a hillside almost 3,500 years ago. Four massive statues of King Ramses II guard the temple.

BARKO'S BLOG-TASTIC EGYPT FACTS

The Great Pyramid at Giza was built around 4,500 years ago as a **tomb** for King Khufu. It is thought to have taken 20 years to build, using an astonishing 2.3 million blocks of stone.

Egypt Fact File

Area: 384,345 square miles
(995,450 square kilometers)

Population: 85,294,388 (July 2013)

Capital city: Cairo

Other main cities: Alexandria; Port Said

Language: Arabic

Main religion: Islam

Highest mountain: Mount Catherine
(8,625 feet/2,629 meters)

Longest river: Nile
(4,132 miles/6,650 kilometers)

Currency: Egyptian Pound

Egypt Quiz

Find out how much you know about Egypt with our quick quiz.

1. What is the capital of Egypt?
a) Luxor
b) Cairo
c) Alexandria

2. Which body of water does the Nile River flow into?
a) Mediterranean Sea
b) Red Sea
c) Lake Victoria

3. What language do Egyptians speak?
a) Portuguese
b) French
c) Arabic

4. Which is the most popular sport in Egypt?
a) soccer
b) baseball
c) tennis

5. What is this?

5. Great Pyramid at Giza
4. a
3. c
2. a
1. b
Answers

29

Glossary

coral reef a long structure made from coral that grows along the coast

felucca a sailing boat

inquisitive being interested in learning about the world

Islam one of the world's main religions; its followers are called Muslims

Marco Polo an explorer who lived from about 1254 to 1324; he traveled from Italy to China

mosque a place where Muslims go to meet and worship

Muslim a person who follows the religion of Islam

oasis a place in a desert where plants can grow because there is water just under the ground

pita bread small flatbread

port a town or city next to a river or the sea, where ships load and unload goods

soap opera a TV program about the lives of a group of characters

souk a busy market with lots of different stalls

tomb a place where a dead person's body is placed

Find Out More

Books

Bojang, Ali Brownlie. *Egypt in Our World*
(Countries in Our World).
Mankato, Minn.: Smart Apple Media, 2012

Heinrichs, Ann. *Egypt* (Enchantment of the World).
New York: Children's Press, 2012

Powell, Jillian. *Egypt* (My Country).
Mankato, Minn.: Smart Apple Media, 2015

Websites

kids.nationalgeographic.com/kids/places
The National Geographic website has lots of
information, photos, and maps of countries around
the world.

www.worldatlas.com
Packed with information about various countries,
this website includes flags, time zones, facts, maps,
and timelines.

Index